T0319193

The Bleeding Heart

THE BLEEDING HEART

and other Poems

Shilia Kaaya

FGD TANZANIA LTD.
P. O. BOX 40331
DAR ES SALAAM, TANZANIA

Published by:
FGD Tanzania Ltd.
P. O. Box 40331
Dar es Salaam, Tanzania
Email: fgdtanzania@gmail.com

ISBN 978-9987-483-10-5

Table of Contents

Dedication

To Kaii
My dearest wife
Having endured
With the strongest of will
Passion and understanding
Shouldering immense responsibilities in my absence

Above all
To Ruth,
Our lovely newly born baby
To whom, I remained a perfect stranger!
To her, I apologize profusely.

Abuja, Not Our Pride[1]

The pain of history manifested
  With shackles of slavery recreated
The wounded lion to slaughter hut
The blunt continent disgusting
With the dirty right in the hut
What a shame and mockery
Not in Berlin or Brussels
But Abuja, Abuja, Abuja.

With the sun never setting
The empire sprawling afar
With Zimbabwe towed to dust
Africa applauding cowardly
With the white commonwealth
Just like the infamous Apartheid
With the elderly Mugabe defiant
And Africa that lame
Out for grab again.

Iron lady then astute
In love with Apartheid
With no hitch or hammer
Africa robbed by day
With the commonwealth smiling
Ian Smith parting with land
Now such a pain to reclaim
With Mugabe pinned to knee.

Though caught with age
And stiff back encroaching
With the economy run down
For touching the godly

---

[1] Reflections on the Common Wealth Abuja Summit, 5 - 8 December
2003 when the issue of Zimbabwe was high in the agender.

Hence the fix and sanctions
With the mass wallowing in pinch
And Museveni was there!
With Mbeki amused!
As Abuja sank low
A shame to Africa
A new epoch indeed
With Nkrumah gone
With Mwalimu gone.

Africa at the Crossroads

The cry of torture
The cry mingled with agony
Of the ambush and surrender
Of the machete or missile
Of the spear or sword
Is a cry all the same.

Africa traumatized
Hacked by treachery
Disguised in the spread of the "word"[2]
Beads and rims of garments.

Africa at the crossroads
As one phase ebbs
Unfolding the ugliest of scenarios
Slavery to colonialism
The pain and shame of Apartheid
Dictatorship and apathy
Now technology and globalisation
All nightmares to mother Africa.

---

[2]   The "word" means the spread of the Word of God as perpoted to be in the Holy Bible.

After Berlin now Brussels

M other Africa, the dream of many
Africa, awash with riches
Africa devoured like a carcass then
Many staring at her
Like greedy hyenas in the Serengeti!

It happened in Berlin
It's 1884, to be precise
Now the shameful balkanization
Looms again,
With viciousness and stubbornness
With arrogance and muscle.

Brussels isn't far from Berlin
The pack of "them!"[3] sat again
With determination, resolve and shamelessness
To slice Africa again.

Thanks, your Excellency, Ben Mkapa
Awakening the giant Africa
Out of a deep slumber
Mugabe isn't the issue
Democracy a mere bait
Africa remains a piece of cake!
For them, not for Africans!

---

[3] "The pack of them" refers to the same group of countries that convened in Berlin in 1884 to partition Africa. The former President of Tanzania Benjamin Mkapa came and clean without missing words that Mugabe wasn't the issue.

Black Gold

Underneath the earth crust
With the swelling womb of fortune
Pregnant with saline and debris
The decomposing dinosaurs
Photosynthesis that captured energy
With bacteria and temperatures
Pressures traversing time and memory
Now the pain of the earth.

Ken Sarowiwa slaughtered
B'cause the riches in the delta
With flames and heat
The black gold to be reached
Through fire or paper
With strife abound everywhere
Not only in Iraq
As Sudan is encroached with ware.

Ancient seas and lagoons the genesis
Mother sun the provider
As the chemistry ensued
Thanks to the bacteria and limestone
The purity of nature amazing
But now the pain persisting
With outcry in Peru and Mexico.

Black coal of industrial revolution
The bowels of the earth remains
The pinnacle of power and policy
And now the black gold
The mother of all pains

With AK 47[4] arrogantly brandished
In the shoulders of teenagers and
mothers
Thrown upon one another
For the black gold to be siphoned.

Blood for Oil!

Blood for oil
As is blood for terror
Weapons of mass destruction
An apparent fools exit
As war rhetoric rumbles
Humanity held ransom
With maniacs of war
Counting the barrels of Oil
Measuring the swelling wombs
The riches of the earth crust.

Oil the secret magic of our times
The key capitalistic dream
Nuclear proliferation the bait
As oil giants consult
Flying across continents
Planning with such mischief
With the scare of war
The world body blackmailed
With pennies and petrol dollars.

The war of shame
That will shed blood for oil

[4] AK 47 - A formidable automatic weapon, invented by a Russian, popularly used now by messionaries and terrorists.

Not for cleansing the humanly filth
Not like lambs sacrifice of the Christians
But humanity ridiculed
Ushering in new era
Of reconstruction and projects.
For the giants and ruthless
Now poised for the kill and profit
Blood for oil a tragedy to the globe
That sits numb in fear of the master
Using the old colonial gimmick
The infamous gunboat diplomacy
Playing fatherly love, vowing to die
Defending humankind to the grave
All sham kindness and concern
As their eyes search the riches of the earth.

Bracing for the Aftermath

New pages of history now unfolding
With the fear gripping even the most astute
What with the world capitals now patronized
By the honest and humble looking missionaries
But their heart pricked and loaded with vengeance
Ready to blow the globe into pieces
Now uncertainty the order of the day
The aftermath so appalling and threatening.

New pages of history now upon us
With reason and wisdom thrown overboard
As cow boy phenomenon now yields poisonous fruits
War front now away from the streets of Baghdad
Mediation ridiculed and a painful mockery now
Bracing for the ugly aftermath the eventuality

As the new order of the world is hatched
From the sinful egg that cracks with such noise.

If wars were the gift of souls
Even paupers would fight with zeal
If suicidal attacks were the gifts hearts
Perverted minds are abundant to exploit
But shedding blood will invite the vengeance of God
If not the curse of the most revered African idols
Directed to perpetrators of war and hatred
With the aftermath now upon us.

The United Nations reduced to a doll
Left to mourn with the rest
Counting the causalities of new order
With the master in the hiding
The ship heading to the deepest of waters
What an appalling aftermath.

And what of Africa
Nairobi in such a mess
Flight cancellation by the colonial master
A death warrant to Mombassa beaches
Tanzania labelled in red
Despite the obedience and diligence
The aftermath to bite dearly
Let's brace for the aftermath ahead.

Seattle, Doha, Finally Cancun![5]

Cancun?
Beautiful and exotic
Endowed beaches rich with healing winds
Romantic with enticing lawns
With the *Mehicos*! Mexico! in tongue
Intriguing smiles; wonderful people
Now Cancun the boiling pot.

Cancun the island to envy
Like Zanzibar the dream of many
And now the heart of many
With the message sent in red
Blood sacrificed in peace and pen
With no bullets but posters of colour.

Cancun beautiful and romantic
With arguments that irritate
Of the sleeping giants creeping to life
Of the masses with noisy empty stomachs
As horses and sheep wallow in butter
Cancun in the heart of heat.

Cancun like a lagoon
From the sky floating in a foam
Lavishly green with cowry shells
Not only for fun and conventions
With the rich flat on sandy beaches
Like ugly lizards basking in the sun
Now terrified of the lingering episode

---

[5]   Reflection on world trade imbalances and global reaction against the suffering facing the poor of the world as a result of the set up. Menstioned are some of the cities whose World Trade Organisation had theirs forums

That engulfed Seattle and Doha.

Seattle, Doha and finally Cancun
Down with agricultural subsidies, tariffs
This tone now for real
Sleeping giants roaring to life.

Clear skies

It is November
Nearing December
Hot and the skies blue
Hot and perspiring
The forecasts faltering
With dust and humid
With the talk of *El-Nino*.

Clouds ebbing
The scorching sun overhead
Banana trees bleaching
With the hurricanes on
Like ghosts of childhood fairy tales
The clear skies terrifying.

It is hot and dusty
With Mount Meru naked
Rivers yawning
Awash with filth and plastic
Not hissing sounds of water
Of the legendary Arusha
Naura and Themi forgotten.

This is The Arusha!
Hot and humid

Dry and tiresome
Stunned with fear
As rains run with winds
Recent phenomenon.

Now colours and festivals
Not only on Saturdays
For the newly weds and lovers
But Sundays and Thursdays
With Fridays to brace
Though hot and humid
Clear skies scary
As Xmas again looms
As we pray for rains.

"Complete Victory!"[6]

With traumatic scenes of death
The earth foundation shaken by tremors
The smoking guns sending shock waves
In pursuit of an illusion
Going for the evil one
Through the havoc of war
With so much love that kills!

"Complete Victory" a must
The lust for peace paraded up front!
Though through wreckage and bombardments
To cleanse the world of the menace

---

6   "Complete Victory"are words uttered by US President, George W. Bush
     refering to the Iraq War, and a war on terror. Complete victory remain a
     mockery to any sensible person.

The weapons of mass destruction
The powders that will visit the veins and nerves
Leading to convulsions and paralysis
The gems so superior to the weaponry at hand
That have flatten Baghdad to the ground
With the beautiful Basra yawning with holes.

"Complete Victory" such an obsession
With the world peace now rented for ever
In witch hunt for peace that is
With so much blood from the innocent
As traces of evidence varnish
May be through the billowing smokes!
From the pounding cluster bombs
Themselves prohibited in lame charters

"Complete Victory" such an illusion
Friendly fire the order of the day
Desperation now taking hold
Though the youth hailed for valour
While others remain engulfed
In the Gulf to win the souls and minds.

"Complete Victory" such a tragedy
With the world fuming with anger
The aftermath beyond comprehension
Though reconstruction such a fortune
Now mechanizations in the corridors
"Complete Victory" at hand!
With the Black Gold underneath!

Crocodile Tears[7]

B asking in the tropical sun
  Rather like a lizard they resemble
With seesaw-like teeth hiding
A log like heap breathing lazily
The crocodile in hiding
Awaiting a plunge into blue waters
With tears to cry!

With tears to cry!
Crocodile tears!
The people of Zimbabwe suffering
Commonwealth agonized
Crying for the Ndebeles and Shonas
As land grab persists
With rigged, sham elections
Tears, crying for the people!

Agile and ferocious in waters
Though eyes watery with tears
With water washing away
The salty poison that is tears
As the wailing sounds of pain echoes
But tears evident
With the jaws closing with might.

Flamboyant gowns blown by wind
Protocol immaculately executed
Torture and amnesty the message
Crying for the mother Africa!
Crocodile tears, salty tears
That washes down the river
As seesaw claws close like ever.

---

[7] Funy that the colonialists have so much love for Zimbabwe!

Like our ancestors of time
Beards and garments thrown around
Now Harare declaration paraded
With Africa fooled to bite
As brethren endure in Zimbabwe
The wrath of a tyranny!
What a blessing from the master
Crying for mother Africa!
Crocodile tears!

Crying for mother Africa

Africa mother of humankind
   Africa the crucible of civilization
But Africa bearing the brunt of pain
As blood spills out of brutal massacres
Now shamelessly engulfing the continent.

Africa mother of humankind
But now the mother of all pains
As the blessed land wrangle with rebellion
An arena for the arsenals
The weapons of terror in the hands
Of the innocent, manipulated child soldiers.

Africa mother of humankind
But abused repeatedly both in mantle and muscle
Her intellect reduced to ridicule
As brethren turn against each other
Up in arms and machete.

Africa mother of humankind
But now caught at cross roads
Siphoning her riches away from her people
Diamonds in Liberia and Siera Leon
The virgin lands of Congo raped viciously.

Africa mother of humankind
Now her soil home to tears
Bodies of the defenceless scattered and buried
Soil to soil the melody of shame
As the globe stare with indifference
As if applauding the genocidal spree.

Africa mother of humankind
But now tearful as betrayal is perpetuated
Its riches the only concern by the rest of humanity
As killing and misery engulf the people
Peace keeping deployment an after thought
The tribal clashes on unabated.

Dark alleys

Through the dark alleys
With ghosts lurking in the darkness
Fear gripping even those in fortress
As secure as the embryonic foetus
With nourishment unsurpassed
As life kicks on like hands of an old clock
With strides that hammer on the earth.

Forces of darkness rumoured
Hacking on the rubble of amour
That has conquered eternity
That cheated even the Vernon

The most virile of poisons
Spited by the condemned sapient.

With the sick mind even sickly
Travelling in distance and time
With resources squandered
What a folly of the mind?
Though eyes sparkle with brilliance
With postures of wisdom and dominance.

Through the dark alleys
Mind clumsy and misty
With death that looms
The evil one reigning supreme!
A frivolity of the sick mind
That sinks that low and blind!

Dense foliage

From the vantage point and posture
Among the lilies of the valley
The hissing sounds of blowsy winds
The cool breeze of dense foliage
That heals the hearts
Awash with medicinal shrines
Its soils sponge and fertile
Virtuous and virgin
My soul wonders while wandering.

Deep in the forest with fen grass
My imagination wanders widely
Steeping down the springs of cold waters
Oozing from the shiny rocks
That remain slippery with moss
Home to life and harmony.

Lost in the forest of variety
With elephant grass and dense forest
The piercing melodies of tiny birds
Thorn birds that steal my heart
My imaginations wander widely
Of the tragedy in making.

Away from noise and filthy
Home to plastic and rusting steel
My soul grieves for the lost glory
As Arusha sinks slowly to slums
With concrete and pavements
That devours foliage and beauty.

In the midst of dust and potholes
Sneaking roads that end nowhere
With hidden mansions of shame
Makeshifts rafters for shelters
That houses the glorified " City dwellers"[8]
The beauty and foliage now folklore.

Dodoma

With time and memories
With resolve and fear
The shadow of Mwalimu looms
Dodoma swarms with heavy weights
Though in patches
Departure such a nightmare.

Since German's tyranny
Dodoma designated the seat

---

[8] "City dwellers" means the contrasts illustrated by quality of houses in our homes - From makeshifts to glass towers.

The route of slave trade
Arid and windy
With people of heart
Though trachoma traumatized.

Dodoma seat of the empire
Though short of fancy and pomp
Now green and flowery
With Chamwino crying for Mwalimu
But Kongwa awash with beef
As the dream remains elusive
Dodoma seat of the empire

Dodoma seat of the empire
Despite feet dragging
Rhetoric that baffles all
With Dar such a magnet
Centre of action, dominating.

Uneconomic they gamble
But Mwalimu will curse
Turning in his grave
His ghost to haunt all.

So Dodoma seat of the empire
Occasionally graced with colours
Powerful motorcades
Sirens and noise
God bless Dodoma
Seat of the empire.

Down the Valley of Death: Walter Sisulu, Bye

The end of the beginning knocking now
With Walter Sisulu back to the dust
A role model of conviction
Shying away from riches
Sacrificing for humanity
And kept behind bars for decades
But emerging the hero of our time.

With Mandela at the infamous Robben Island
Enduring humiliation with courage
Walking down the valley of death together
Defiant of the shameful Apartheid regime
Vowing to die for the cause
Inspiring the mass of oppressed afar
Far beyond the land of Shaka.

Down the valley of death
With other freedom fighters brutalized
Walter Sisulu walked steadily
Though in prison for life
With ANC[9] of his age deep in heart
With Oliver Tambo in the run
Guiding the cause to finality
Now Walter Sisulu the icon to emulate
Though age has taken toll with impunity.

Though we part with you pained immensely
You remain the pillar of history
As the new generation fumbles with forgetfulness

---

[9]   ACN - African National Congress.

The enemy hiding in the darkness
Indulgence to riches now the focus of shame
With our people still in the shackles of poverty
Your revolution threatened and encroached to
With the continent now ever engulfed
With the enemy in the most sophisticated of combats
Poised for a final kill
Walter Sisulu we salute you
May your soul rest in peace.

Finally Victory

Height of absurdity?
People making a choice?
Between a hoax and substance?
Of colonialism, of impending balkanization?
Of neocolonialism dressed elegantly
In the attire "democracy!"

Oppression manifests itself
Not only in one dimension
It comes in camouflages
In hiding and rhetoric
In scorn and arrogance.

Bravo Africa!
The giant Africa we salute you
For uttering in unison
Seeing the light, seeing the sham
Saying no, no!
Let them change the venue
Spain may appeal now
In pursuance of their agenda

That binds them together
"The Common Interests"[10]
Reaching down to the bowels of Africa
Milking her pale and thin.

Fists of Support[11]

With the strongest valour
    Man's vengeance against oppression
Oppression in its multiple facets
The brutal stumble over expressions
The block against freedom
Over racial divide
Springs from beneath the wounds of suffering.

But we have this revealed
In the secret of history
The legend of man's survival
Against the bouts of intimidations
That man cares for his manness.

He judges rains from heavy clouds
And curses the colourful rainbow
He responds to the hearty smile
But the twisted ones deserve doubts.

This perception is the gift of man
And is there to stay
The feelers of imaginations explore
Roaming like antennae of a cockroach

---

[10] "The common interests" an auphanism on the fact that what blinds the
west in not the love for Africa but its wealth.

[11] Reflection on the error of apatheid, written during my high school and
college days, late eighties and nineties.

A fragment of bread speaks
Its own language to the lowly
Hungry and nocturnal cockroach.

Not only the black
But also all the people of colour possess this magic
They can never be blinded
That the leopard is a lamb
Its tail will always poke out
From the majestic shrewd of the lambs skin.

Our support from this end
Over the impending elections
May you triumph over the hoax?
As we brandish our fists of support
And cry for the sustained struggle.

Flying[12]

Flying is magical
   Care and attention skills refined
Smiles and professional gestures
A menu of steadiness
On board the vessel
Above the cloud
Beyond the blue sky.

Air hostess in uniforms
Alert and caring
Tenderly and inspiring
Welcome aboard.

---

[12]   Based on actual experience when the plane I was flying with experienced
landing difficulties.

Then the landing nightmare
The roof of Africa visible
Protruding above the clouds
Much like an iceberg of the North Sea
And the clouds as dense
With fog mingled with rains
The landing strip in hiding.

Then the calm voice
The captain speaking
With panic setting in
With images of MV Bukoba
With prayers in silence.
Even for atheists
The hissing sound of broken hearts
Closer to Thee!
Despite the pilots calmest of voices
That flying back an option
If landing finally futile.

Flying is magical
But also loathsome
When landing turns a nightmare
With souls full of sorrow.

Follow the Mountain, the Beauty

Away from the dust
The smoke and noise
The hectic city "the haven of peace"[13]
Vanishes from the vicinity
As we meander and ride
Bending with blow and speed
The elephant grass and palm trees.

It is March nearing April
The rains abound
And greenery splendid
The road to Arusha
To the far away lands
Signals with mirage.

Dar, Kibaha, Chalinze
Cautious! The white hats!
Check speed or part with a buck
Over speeding a feast to them!

It is green and beautiful
The flowers blossom and Sparkle
Vast lands unfold
As we slowly approach
The meandering Wami
With stories of crocodile and teeth.

From the coast line
With sand and humidity
Hot and suffocating
To altitude and longitude
Follow me,
Follow the mountain

means Dar es Salaam.

Follow the beauty
Come to the climax of creation.

Travel by day and marvel
At what nature radiates
Tenderly and majestically.

As you approach the Usambaras
The imposing earth crusts
With beauty and wonder
The Pare mountains parade in row
Inviting and enticing
Challenging one to dare scale them!

The lilies of the valley
The flowers that blossom,
The baobab with big heart
On the slopes of Kilimanjaro.

Lift your eyes, bless your heart
The roof of Africa visible
The Twin Mountains glitter
The double-peaked Kilimanjaro
The majestic Meru
Karibu Arusha
The " *Geneva of Africa*"[14].

---

[14]   When the former US President Bill Clinton was in Arusha to attend Broad Peace Negotiation (BPN) meeting at AICC in 2002, he could not resist to express the beauty of Arusha, and the best description he came up with was calling Arusha - The Geneva of Africa!

Get Hold of Your Peace

There is no peace
Peace is as elusive
As the shifting sand dunes
Of the Sahara and Kalahari deserts
Peace sits in the mind
Dwelling in the heart of man.

Life is worthless
In the absence of peace of mind
One's composure is
Wrapped in the peace of mind
And peace is life
Even to the impoverished
Even to the lame
The causalities of history
Peace restores the sense of life
Though in agony and pains
Get hold of your peace.

"Global Apartheid"[15]

History vocabularies
Speak of the limping globe
Injured by injustice
Torn apart by egocentrism
That enriches the select
Just pockets of humankind.

The shackles of industrial revolution
Set pace if not copied
The land monopoly of history
That created empires
Where the sun had never to set!

Then followed exportation of terror
Disruption of harmony
The links, similarities
Patterns evident
As the world suffers
From one form of misery
To the deadliest of all
Now renamed *"global Apartheid"*.

The vessels of misery
Come in colours and style
Protocol signed in futile
With conditionality and ties
Good governance now the key word
Kyoto protocol redundant

---

[15] "Global Apartheid" a buzzword that has evolved to describe a new global paradigm. It is an international system of minority rule that promotes inequality, disparities and different access to basic human rights, wealth and power. It is the opposite of global democracy. You can find more on this if you read Pambazuka News, September 9, 2004 by Charles Mutasa.

With the biggest polluter
Laughing at a distance!
The suffering continues
The patterns ever the same
Entrenched now by globalization.

Happy Chameleon

Her motion lingers in pace
Eyes rolling and bulging
Its head blunt and ugly
Hesitant in approach
Though with a firm tail
That coils in style
Gripping the tender tendrils.

Master of camouflage
Not only in colours
But motion that disguises
With a tongue that flings
Incapacitating the prey.

And happy is the chameleon
Though slow in motion
Gifted with eyes
As big as fish eyes in the pond
Or hawks that terrorize from the sky
And the slow motion
A mimicking motion.

Floundering in the clear
With no mud or flood

Though the foliage dense
Blending with the fragile frame
The permeating rays blended
As chameleon changes colour
Out to suffocate the termite
Happy chameleon in hiding
Though visible and ugly.

Think of the chameleon
Not the loveliest of creatures
From childhood my agony
Though not her pray
Not like a fly
But my body remains chilly
Thinking of the ugly chameleon
Clinging on my back
May be by mistake.

Hold On Winnie (The Good Old Days)[16]

When the racists snatched me from you
I saw a ball of tear running down your chick
You wept with the strongest agony
And shook with rage of anger and love.

The day of separation
But yet the day of intimacy
The great day
The great day Winnie
Even in our new home the "cell".

---

[16] Written based on imagination when Nelson Mandela was still imprisoned.

Yes, Winnie
This is no illusion
But a body less reality
I feel you beside me
With your strong arms
Pillowing my head.

Thank you my love
For the real love
For you love humanity
And you love the love
For humanity is love.

My heart is burning with love
My heart full of ghostly dreams
Of the beautiful land
The land beyond the hills
The land of love.

And up the hill we shall climb Winnie
Up to the summit
And down to the other side
To scenery and grassy land
The land of love.

Hold on Winnie
Hold on my darling
The jewel of my soul
Till the dawn of victory.

I See Lumumba; I Cry

I see Lumumba
My tears trickle down
I see Mwalimu
My heart burns with pain
As Nkrumah floats
In the blue cloudy skies
Africa now ripe for the filth!
What a pain, what a pain
Stive Biko bruises still fresh, gushy.

I see Lumumba; my soul torn asunder
Not for Africa; too volatile a son
Not for Africa; Her destiny hijacked
With crocodile tears in gushes
Ridiculing Africa of her heroes
Ian Smith, darling of the west.

I see Lumumba, I sob, I cry
Shamelessly they grabbed him
Disgrace on their faces,
Not a trace of shame, sinners!
Leading him to the darkness
With Mobutu in the shadows
As Idd Amin sends shivery
The strategy running sour
See! The savages of Africa!

Then came Mandela
The gift of humankind
With heart that big and soft
A condemned terrorist!
Cry mother Africa
Your womb cursed from birth.

I see Lumumba, I sob, I cry
Tears roll down my cheeks,
Soft and tender
Courage to give me
Strength to renew
Till the day I dry tears
Tears of the downtrodden.

Is Good Governance the Issue?

The slogan now goes
With good governance
The good books open for you
With democracy of prescription
You're lauded and praised
The model in Africa
The qualifier to the next release.

Good governance now a song
With lessons of Mobutu forgotten
Savimbis now history in archives
Though the darling of the west
The heroes of time
Conduit for the riches.

Africa evolving
With rebirth of the concept
As if Nkrumah didn't envision it!
As if Nyerere didn't leave it!
AFRICA UNION KARIBU
Though a mockery to Bush
With Madagascar the first test.

The formula stark clear
Discard the spent forces
Mobutu and the like

Had outlived their values
And replacements a necessity
With the bowels of Africa still lavish
With gold and glittering diamond.

With abundant oil on the ocean shores
Emerging fortunes
The changing patterns
That never change
Permanent interest their policy!

Nobel Laureate - Jimmy Carter

Jimmy Carter the family man
Though lustful in heart
His flesh remained restrained
Shying away from pride
And the pomp of super presidents
And now a Nobel Laureate.

In human rights a firm believer
Human rights an inventor of nations
And not the contrary
Recounting the pain of America
Now reeling in pain
In the darkest of all times.

Carter once narrated of weak person
As analogues of weak nation
That crosses it hands
Neglecting humanly gestures
Behaving with bluster
Boasting with rashness
Not knowing of insecurity
That the insanity depicts.

Human rights he sung
The soul of nationhood palpating
Echoing beyond seas and horizons
And the safety of human kind.

In Tanzania an adored folk
With "*Sasakawa Global 2000*"[17]
Imprinted in the heart of people
On the roof of Africa he stood
As he scaled with passion and love
The Kilimanjaro, pride of Africa.

And recently with guts and wisdom
Lamenting on the seeds of war
Warning of the disintegrating globe
With dialogue and patience ebbing
Ushering in muscle and arrogance
In the hands of lunatics of our times.

Kilimanjaro Bleeds for the Earth

A century ago Kilimanjaro stood its ground
With glaciers a mile deep and spackling
The famous landmark for Africa
But now the thermometer
The palpating heart of creation bleeding
The natural indicator of the decomposing earth.

Kilimanjaro the pride of Africa

---

[17] "Sasakawa Global 2000"An international Green Program sponsored by
the formaer US President Jimmy Carter aimed at reducing hunger in
Africa. Tanzania was one of the beneficiary countries especialy in maize
production.

Kilimanjaro the climax of beauty
Towering high on the African skyline
Beating the scotching heat of the equator
Cooling the thirst of many
But now on the verge of disaster
Hatched by the spoiler
The man with his infamous civilization.

Global warming the instrument
The vessel industrialization on high seas
Massive deforestation in Brazil
Amazon and Congo forests raped
Their virginity abused with such ferocity.

Kilimanjaro bleeds for the earth
With her glaciers evaporating
Her charm and beauty endangered
Tourists to lament
Tanzania, Africa in tears and sorrow
As the pride of Africa shrinks
Reeling in pain and agony
As the virus engulfs
Sneaking in with malice
With the massive exploitation of the earth
Its resources irreplanisheable though.

Mandela[18]

They may temper with your body
They may inject you with a virus
That ruins the body of man
But that only does one thing
Tell what villains they're
Boers are stiff foolish
A mass of stinking garbage
A most degenerate species of mankind
For hammering on a rock
Our rock Mandela
Whatever they do to you
Makes no difference, dear
You remain the foundation
And a rock indeed
Of our aspirations and destiny.

Manyara, Now Eternal[19]

Welcome history
Manyara of flamingos
Manyara a lake in danger
At times covered by sand
That signals afar
Of the eminent danger
Of disappearance.

---

[18] Written *(8th August 1988)* when Mandela fell sick while still in jail, Robben Island, and had to undergo lung operation.

[19] Reflection on the scenerios leading to creation of Manyara as the newest Region in Tanzania.

Manyara now eternalized
Manyara of dimension by division
Manyara born of division
That was preceded
With labour pains if not anguish
Welcome Manyara
The region in making.

Arusha was vast in expanse
Hours of distance to cover
Rift valley a region rumoured
Of cattle and donkeys
Of huge farms and hoes
Of language and features
Of culture and civility.

Division frantically discussed
What of Ngorongoro?
The pride of Africa
What of the "Geneva of Africa?"
National unity ignored
Tribalism and triviality
Assuming the centre stage.
Suddenly the labour pains over
The debate halted with honour
As baby Manyara is born
Now grasping for air
With the first piercing cry
Of a newly born baby
Welcome aboard
26th region, Manyara.

Memories of Childhood

From fussy myopic images
  Of glorified gigantic structures
With spoons so big and heavy!
Daddy and mom ultimate fences
As secure as anything even
In the den of death, danger looming.

With river gorges deep and terrifying
The sky spackling with stars
God seated on the shaded moon
With eyes rolling out and fearful
Don't you ever swear in God's name!

The stories, the stories! Fairy tales
Our Maasai Uncle from Ngorongoro
Out in the run from famine
With flocks of cattle, sheep and goats
His donkeys cracking dry studs
With us kids seated on the dust
Listening but trembling with fear.

Coming of age a nightmare
Story telling a merry wish
Swearing in God's name the trick
As fairy tales forbade
Wish one would remain a baby
Sucking on a finger with fantasies
With illusions of mighty daddies.

Mererani in Tears, Bye Mkalama[20]

The blue rock sought by heart
With heart breaking news
That left many asunder
With tears and misery
Of memories and agony.

With the El-nino still vivid in mind
Death by suffocation and anguish
Of filthy water and debris
Now of compressor and poisonous gas
At Block B of wealth and value
But also of greed and shame.

Martin Adam Mkalama I cried for you
With your picture engrossed on your coffin
With you coiled there incognito
Singida, Makiba and Mikungani
Yes, Mbuguni, Tengeru, Usa River
Down town Arusha with friends in tears
Bye bye MKALAMA and group
May your souls rest in peace.

---

[20] Friends and foes died during this traumatic experience. That included my schoolmate at Mikungani Primary school in Mbuyuni, very close to the mining area. I attended the funeral.

Mount Meru This Morning

It is another beautiful morning
The blue skies clear
Prelude to the nasty day unfolding
With rains still a parable
Not impressive
Not at all.

Driving down this tarmac road
Mind clumsy and tired
As Eid- El-Fitr shifts like mirage
With paper work awaiting
Next day off indeed
To celebrate the end of fasting.

Cold breeze blazing through
Staring through the window
Mind reflecting wondering
As my soul is stolen
By the breath taking scenery
Imposing Mount Meru glittering.

Oh! not like everyday
The towering peak in crystals
Sparkling white with snow
Hope you see it too
What a contradiction!
It is still dry and hot.

Snow filling the gorges
Eyes pained by the sparkle
As temptation irks me
Thinking of the roof of Africa
Now lying behind my back

The snowy Kilimanjaro
Though now bleeding.

Wish it were raining
For Mount Meru to glitter
With ice and snow
Like this morning
As I stare at her
Longing for the rains.

Mount Meru: The Lost Glory

Mount Meru of rain and beauty
Mount Meru the jewel of Arusha
The snowy cape on occasion
The majestic protruding rock
A mass of forest and elephant grass
The envy of admiring visitors.

The roots of the mountain buttressed
So admirably to Mbuguni plains
Closer to the blue rock, Tanzanite
Flowing to Engarenanyuki of history
Where the Meru warriors clashed
With the landgrabbers of time
With "*Bwana Shauri*"[21] ordering fire
Putting aflame the homesteads
Leaving people destitute and in tears
Painfully narrated in "Blood on our land"
In childhood memories of Ismael Mbise
One of our sons caught in the web of boers

---

[21]   *Bwana Shamba* - Area Agricultural Officer

In pursuit of green pastures
Like the salty grass and waters
Of the legendary Waato River.

Mount Meru abused
Stripped naked by machete and seesaw
Cutting down the Loliondos
"*Mfumu*"[22] waiting in awe
Having sacked to death the "*Nseseve*"[23]
Now waiting for her turn
From the merciless, the greedy man
With motor engine and haulage lorries

Rivers thirsty and cursing
Abundant water a lost glory
As Naura and Themi yawn with rubbish
Marlboros and filthy
With houses of shame to river beds
The glory of Mount Meru lost forever.

---

[22] *Mfumu* is a parastic type of tree which attaches to another type of tree *Nseseve* and eventualyy grows into a huge tree suffocating the other tree to extinction.

[23] Nseseve is a host tree that is eventually suffocated by the invited tree to death

Interpretation: In Kimen folklore, invited colonialists ended up wanting to throw our people out of our land.

My Fate

I know what awaits me
The ruthless battalion on cover
Fearing the outburst of my anger
And yet bold enough
To spring on to me.

I know the fate of my survival
And the central dogma of my being
I know my route at the cross roads
And will never mistake it
For the enemy's camouflaged one.

I know the sorrow of manhood
And the cornerstone of my happiness
And for it I shall fight
Till the dawn of victory
Or the dusk of death.

I am armed with the lion's courage
The spirit to remain aflame
Through the days of massacre
Through the days of bloodshed
To the day of victory.

I remain the son of war
Which is the asylum of my fate
In face of the mutineer
And dehumanized racists.

But I shall fight in mute
With the mystical powers
Of my people's rights
Filling me with boldness
And sacred to win.

Let them kill my body
Satisfy their primitive desires
Of oppression and humiliation
In the mere dreams of vainness.

My soul will roam
In the townships of Soweto
Go over the Table Mountains
and beyond
Holding the spear of Shaka high
And fight ceaselessly
The war of liberation.

From the cell of suffering
I salute all freedom fighters
With my "brothers in fate" oath aflame
In the name of freedom and unity
And may God bless our struggle.

Notes:
These were imagined feelings of Nelson Mandela then (1988)
while still in Prison at the Robben Island.

Next Dawn

*D*ays count by click
   From dawn to dusk
With the golden sky afar
Shaded rays filtering
Through the foliage and clouds
Of muted cries and grieving silence.

From the dawn to the dusk
With darkness engulfing the globe
The next dawn such a nightmare
With intrigues and mechanizations
Of the hideous schemes.

With the golden sky afar
Sleepless night of ghostly dreams
With silence so scary and terrifying
Giants fusing and embracing
What of the next dawn.

Shaded rays filtering
With history such a tyranny
Wounds to be licked like salt
With the golden dusk just a reminder
Next dawn, next dawn coming!

Through the foliage and clouds
Of the earth that bleed with blade
Of the star wars to fight the aliens
With the world left with pain
Next dawn such a nightmare
Muted cries and grieving silence
Of the midnight fever and anguish
As times flies over

Next dawn I hate you
Next dawn I curse you
The morning sunrise mourning
Not a blessing of the sunshine!

Next Front, Water Blues

Like the sun and air
Like algae and moss on rocks
With camels that persevere
Or the lizards of Kalahari
Water the link to life.

Like the sun and air
Water in its purity and sanctity
In glaciers and rivers of history
With the Nile meandering like a snake
Life and civilization is water
Still in vaults of earth crusts for life
Though scant and salty for thirsty
And now the next front in the making.

Like algae and moss on rocks
Or the dinosaurs that roamed the earth
Vanishing like vapour with heat
With Sahara spreading in hips of dunes
Is water vanishing in haste?

Not like diamonds and slaves
That fattened America and Albion
Not like black gold and ivory
With ivory towers pleandour
That the west cherishes as riches
From Africa and afar

Water blues the final front
That will shed blood profusely.

Not like the intrigues of commerce
Much like the ancient merchants of Venice
Water there for humankind
Not metric kilos to count
Or replenish like the lust for power
That leaves the globe bleeding
God forbade this front
For life is that sweet
And water is life.

On Globalization

A century ago and down the memory lane
With the rise and fall of civilizations
With the conquest of empires
Others from mere bellowing trumpets
The pace of change engulfed the world
The semblance of globalization took root.

Germans with ferocious firepower
And the British with their cunning smiles
Vasco Dagama in imposing amour attire
History shaped by adventures of the high seas
Maps drawn on the black continent
Distance and tsetse fly the felony
Inhibiting the exploits and excitement.

Shaka rose in arms, Mkwawa picking the melody
Majimaji uprising up in black magic
The fight finished by Mwalimu

Though his hands remained closely tied
With the world of tariff and imbalances
Masters still at the helm
But now the terrain so difficult
The globe such a small village
History that repeats shamefully upon us
The tricks ever the same but more refined.

The globe woven in such an intricate cobweb
The buttons pressed with precision
Either bulging to gimmick or perish in explosion
Competing with the giants and powerful
Darwinian theory now taking hold
The arena so insecure and uneven.

Globalization an unpleasant reality
Learning the magic the only orifice
The only escape though crowded with hitches
With control held with such a grip
Breaking free not a fancy affair
May God Bless the lowly not only in magic!
As the patterns evolve evoking the memories
The History that remains ever painful.

Patterns

*D*ar then the hub of liberation
     Mazimbu, Kongwa, Nkrumah Street
Nyerere the icon burning with desire
Colonial bondage the pain, the anguish.

Memories rekindled,
Kawawa now agile
Diamond Jubilee flocked
Emotions running high
Zimbabwe simmering with crunch
The master avenging.

Bismarck diplomacy runs amok
Bow or break
The pack singing in unison
Africa at the cross roads.

It is now or never
As the python coils back
The patterns ever the same
May be Dar has spoken
GOD bless Africa.

People, Planet, Prosperity: Reality or Rhetoric?

In Rio –Brazil they met in style
The top brass of the world convened
Resolving in earnest
Though with reluctance
That People, Planet, Prosperity the Agenda.

Ten years down the line
The globe bleeds profusely
Of deforestation and poisonous gases
Of the yawning ozone layer
Of nuclear proliferation
Of the widening poverty gap.

People, Planet, Prosperity a mockery
With the Earth Summit singing again
Agenda 21 a glaring rhetoric
Ridiculed by the powers that are
With five minutes of stammering speech
And the shameful non-attendance
Of the mighty and powerful.

People, Planet, Prosperity rhetoric
To be sung by the impoverished
Dreamed of by the down trodden of the Earth
Squeezed further to marginalization
Bolted on ground by globalization
Welded to steel by trade tariff by the West
And notorious subsidy for the rich!
Despite the outcry and misery
That the world suffers, endures.

Rio, now Johannesburg bursting to capacity
With people of race and gender
With people of good will and wishes
Of rosy dreams and fantasies
Of the just world
That remains a pipe dream!

Poetry

Armed with a pen and ink
Mind that blinks with wit
Time and space the limit
Venting poison the Vernon.

Searching souls and hearts
Healing wounds and bruises
Though pricking with agitation
With emotions that will kill
Poetry the vehicle of vengeance.

Poetry the treasure of wisdom
Its life spanning evolution
Its voice smoothing like oil
That anointed kings of empires
Poetry the mother of all art.

Poetry the song of war
Its prowess the sword that kills
Its melody without a parallel
With poets the pain in the flesh
Their poetry the gift of time.

Poetry the universal vessel
Its seats the comfort of aliens
Despite the turbulence and siege
With life the precious choice
Poetry the heart of hearts.

With trumpets that bellow
Up the hills and down the valleys
Across seas and oceans of dreams
Poetry transcends boundaries
Poetry magical and universal.

Prayer for Sanity

Before thy eyes and mercy
With eyes blinking with pain
Souls ghostly in such sorrow
As catastrophe mutes in earnest
With the sun set approaching
With flashes of fire from gunshots.

Before thy eyes and mercy
Hearts bleeding and weighty
Redeem us from the evil grip
From the hands of the evil one
With blood trickling not for salvation
Not for heavenly sanctification
But the greed and Armageddon.

Before thy eyes and mercy
Redeem us from evil mind
That bows before you with malice
With prayers and attire
The high priest and messengers of peace
But alas! The Angels of death.

Before thy eyes and mercy
Redeem humankind from treachery
From the lambs skin wearers
The saintly pretenders with veto
Or with rage and vengeance
Thence the suffering
That spreads by day.

Before thy eyes and mercy
For lies and treachery you forbade
Broken hearts and watery eyes

With echoing cries in Gaza Strip
Sacred soils socked with blood
May the coming dawn unfold peace
Anointing justly, God fearing Kings.

September 11ᵗʰ

The date tainted with blood
The date that shed tears
Left humankind horrified
And perplexed beyond limit.

September 11th a shame to mankind
The climax of the ugliest of deeds
That humankind can breed
Driven by selfishness and malice.

The genesis not withstanding
Wounded the world is
Shame upon civilization
And a mockery to humanity
Though a lesson, if ever one
A bitter way indeed.

September 11th a scaring blemish
A reminder of immorality
That drives the world
As wealth is pursued with impunity
With viciousness and arrogance.

People blown to pieces and flesh
With glasses scattered afar
Souls suffocating
Under debris of steel and smoke

With the Twin Towers of pride
Crumbling to a heap
That remains cursing the evil one
With hands, fingers
Dripping of innocent blood
May it never happen again
Not again anywhere.

Sokoine, the Son of Africa

The news struck like thunderbolt
Shattering and crumbling my being
Pounding on to me
In a way not to express.

Tears welled from my eyes
Like blood from a punctured artery
Who could stand it?
A man of what wit and clout?

I cried with sorrow and bitterness
And nobody could stop me
I felt the pinch tearing my soul
As the news echoed
From my "*dudu*"²⁴ proof radio.

How could I shake it out of my mind?
Empty it somewhere remote
And restore the peace of my mind.

---

24 A simplistic radio made for the purpose of famers and low - income earners in Tanzania whose functioning was easily broken down once an insect *dudu* like a cockroach finds its way into the radio.

So, man passes like a flower
Today he glows in full bloom
Tomorrow he wrinkles like an aged fossil
Today he is full of vigour
Tomorrow he bears the most sorrowful look
That is a long legend of life
And the secret of man's fate and vitality.

An inevitable path it is
To be followed by father and son
Mother and daughter not to deviate from
The whole mankind is haunted by it
As it boasts in naked mercilessness
Today and tomorrow
And the infinite time to come.

It is the day that comes in secrecy
Conquering in havoc
Claiming victory in abundance of strength
And considers no age and fame
This day I resent and hate
But remains my bosom part
Striking when it strikes.

But then I rebuked it
12th April 1984, for what it did
Inflicting the worst it could
Imposing emptiness and sorrow
And for that I hate it today
Though I stare at it in awe.

He was a man of great destiny
A man never to fade in our memory
A man of the people
Truly beloved son of Africa
Edward Moringe Sokoine.

Though in body we lost you
Your legacy lives, lingers on
Your commitment remains admirable
Your dedication enshrined in history.

Lest we forget you, the immortal
Though it hurts to remember
May Almighty God bless you
May you find a place in eternal bliss.

Soldier's Soul and Mind

Clad in combat and weaponry
With blowsy winds that terrify
Ghostly beaded shadows looming
Teenagers scared to the guts
Chasing the fathoms of illusions.

Only recently Jimmy flown home
His casket clad with colours of the nation
With a hero's salutation awaiting him
Though his mother crying bitterly
With Doris dreams shattered forever
My soul and mind clouded with dreams
Wish was home with mom and safe.

With bombs now rocking Baghdad
Though the war is over!
If not for the bloody Syria!
No, No, all of them
But poor me
Embroiled in dreams and fantasies.

Wish was in Harvard with them
Sharpening my wit with knowledge
As deals hatch by day
With me in war and stupid
Wish was home with Mom and Daddy.

Standing here!
Standing here!
Damn me!
Damn me!
Wish was home with Mom and Daddy.

Stive Biko Remembered

The stark brutality shocked all
Steve Biko hacked to death
Bruised from balm to head
Wounded only in body
But his soul triumphed over the merciless
torture.

Heaped by shameless torturers
To the back of the police van
Paraded naked in the chilling cold
Of the winter that sprawled afar
From Port Elizabeth to Pretoria
In such pain and anguish.

His sin denouncing dehumanization
His fatal error daring to speak
That infamous Apartheid a menace
That Black Consciousness our refute
The Pride of the Black Man.

Stive Biko son of the soil
Your footprints engraved in fire
Your tears the seeds of victory
Your heart the house of hope
Guiding us through peril
Fighting to honour you earnestly.

Quarter a century in time and space
Your ideas speak loud and clear
Our destiny, our fate
The weapon you spoke of then
Remains the weapon today
That "the oppressed mind" own sword
Gripped firmly by "the oppressor".

Steve Biko remembered
25 years on and up
The struggle continues
May your soul rest in peace.

Sunrise Beauty

Crawling out for the morning walk
My eyes sleepy and tired
Yawning after such slumber
My eyes edging the easterly horizon
As clouds ebb with a release
Clearing the phenomenon hatch
The morning sunrise.

Far away
Beyond the reach of the roof of Africa

While Mount Meru remains hidden
Walking down this rough road
Banana leaves swaying with a breeze
With coffee tree still abundant
The marvel I crave for
As slums encroach in haste
This greenery …this greenery
My mind wonders.

And then the earth hatching in style
From the far eastern horizon
Bursting out like a ball
As I stare in awe and marvel
With the golden sky dominating
Look! Look! It is early in the morning
With such a blessing in the offing
The morning sunrise.

Strolling down the slippery road
Thanks God for the gift of rain
After such a drought and strain
Now greenery and breeze
And this beauty indeed
The sunrise beauty
From the far eastern horizon
Happy New Year.

Terror in the Horizon

The world in its toes
Conventional armoury faltering
Common sense irrational
Acts of terror in the rise

Mass causalities now the concern.
The genesis of war, of terror
The roots of fear and hate
Has a safe asylum in the sick minds
Deploying the religious gimmick
Loud mouthing globalization
Free market and mobility
All reinventing the history
That has remained ugly and painful.

The pattern crystal clear
From slavery to colonialism
The class society of shame
That ushered in the tragedy of Apartheid
Now fundamentalism for defence
Dar, Nairobi, September 11th
Mombasa of late and the impending fear.

Terrorism not an invention
But the dimension and direction yes
Touching the untouchables
Hence the deafening outcry
The enclave leaking and dented
Safety jeopardized
Terror in the horizon
Fear now unleashed
Praying together for wisdom
That humankind glues together
In concerted efforts, healing the sick minds.

The African Child

Children the blessing of life
Their laughter the envy of many
Their cry the sign of health
Their misery the pain of pairs.

Children the biblical models
Heavens moulded on their stature
Their dreams the oil of life
Their love limitless and colour blind.

Children the gift of life
Their pain the shame of life
Their bruises the curse of generations
Sharperville massacre a dark spot
Such a shameful commemoration!

Cries of torture tormenting melodies
Though Soweto destined to history
Child solders now the dirtiest of
creations
As lust for power overpower the powerful
Child labour such an absolute monster.

Children of the world the feast of sinners
Rape and filthy the awful headlines
Streets souls a hatching phenomenon
That will rock nations to knees
Child abuse such an abomination.

The Amazing Ngorongoro

Going down to the bowels of the earth
Down to the alkaline Malakat Lake
The depression, the caldera
Close to the colourful flamingos
The "*big five*"[25]
Rhinos and lionesses, the hunter
The hunters and the hunted
The coward hyena with iron teeth
The fat hippos, fearful of the scotching sun
What a treasure
What a gift to mankind.

The amazing fauna
Virgin flora
The deep forest of variety
The beaded trees!
With long faces like
hidden eyes of
The creator, the Maker.

The stupid Rhino
Of the erotic love fantasies in oriental
Of the magical armoury value
For the rich Arabs of the Emirates
With sickly memory
The splashing urinator
The black rhino, what an awesome sight!
What a heap of life
For admiration and wonder.

---

[25] "big five" refers to the most famous wild animals found in our national parks, they include Lion, Elephant, Leopard, Buffalo and Rhino.

Ngorongoro amazing
May you live and flourish
Conquering eternity
Stirring humanity to sense
For respect and perfect harmony.

The cloud, the mist
The singing thorn birds
The deafening silence
The chilly morning
Of fog and darkness
Ngorongoro a marvel
The unparalleled wonder.

The "GARDEN OF EDEN"[26]
The cradle of mankind
The stunning climax of creation
Where man and nature coexist
With restraint and respect
The Maasai of flamboyant attire
Of relic, the jumping music
Dance and folklore
Ngorongoro unique
Ngorongoro amazing.

The Ashes of Carlson: for ex-Ilborians

Familiar faces met happily
Others limping of age if not gout!
While others stared at each other
Mesmerized by the reunion
Brought about by unique love

---

[26]   The biblical mentioned garden, purpotedly the most beautiful garden

Ushered in by no one else
But Steward Gustav Carlson.

Steward Gustav the pride of all
The mentor at Ilboru
His magical charm activated
His confident walk and stroll
As captivating and fresh in memory
His love for soil rekindled
His familiar shouts echoes again
"Stockings up!"[27] some remember
Now his ashes such a blessing.

Stewart Gustav Carlson
The role model in leadership
From the steering position and power
To loyalty and obedience
To his own student of pride
Dr. AnzaAmen Lema of wisdom.

Carlson decreed in will
Vowed his part to rest at Ilboru
To nurse his plants of variety
For his botany classes of success
That held many captive
Enticing Dr. Urasa to the novelty
Of science and professional discourse.

Carlson a legend and myth
His love for Africa exemplary
His ashes now in rightful place
Witnessed proudly and in tears

[27] Thought not an ex-Ilborian and indeed not belonging to that generation, I loved not to resist to be enticed by stories on this hugely popular Headmaster who had won so much admiration. "Stockings up" was just one of his popular orders requiring students to remain smart.

By young lions of his creation
That now steer the nation
To the heights of achievement.

The Ball of Fire

Why the talk of war
The memories of Hiroshima
The tough stance and arrogance
Of power and muscle.

The world now hanging on balance
With the talk of war
Of terrorism and antiterrorism
Of massacre and blood shed
With wisdom thinning
The language of wisdom ridiculed.

Human casualty the order of the day
Justification for bombing sought by heart
In the name of vengeance and revenge
The right of survival a key word
As if Darwin was resurrected
To teach the lesson afresh.

The capacity for the final crunch evident
In the hands of the craziest of them
All labelled in names
But yet fateful to all mankind.

The danger looms high
The smoking guns and rockets leveled
Others dreaming of "Armageddon"

The globe suspended, afloat
Crossing the smoky sky
As a fateful ball of fire.

The Beautiful Flower

*D*espite man's destructive mind
   Along with his evil ideas
His blind expeditions
Cutting down traces of living
Suppressing the essence of humanity
Ignoring the sweetness of peaceful life
He shall one day come to a stand still.

His surprise will come like thunder bolt
His motives vanishing like fat over fire
For the right shall prevail
Suppressing brutality and villainy
His ideas put to grave
For victory will shine
Stubbornly standing clear of destruction
A simple but true victory.

It is the end of oppression
A new page for genuine progress
That will glitter like the morning sun
And rejoice like the beautiful flower
A flower from the remnants
Of man's destruction.

That is the flower out of bloodshed
A true flower any way
With all its lovely colours and scent
The flower in black and white

The flower in red and pink
The flower in blue of the heaven
The flower in the mighty golden blend
The colours of butterfly
And blessed is this colourful flower.

The Blackman in Peril

Think of the genesis of human kind
Think of the roots of life in Olduvai Gorge
Think of Africa that spans the length of the globe
Africa that towers high with the gift of Kilimanjaro
Africa awash with wealth and value
Africa bounced on by vultures in pursuit of her riches
Africa smeared with blood as her diamonds vanish
Africa of the vast Sahara desert
That was once dense with foliage and black "*mpingo*".[28]

Think of the Blackman in peril
The inventor and gold smith before the dawn
The magicians who baffled even the legendary Mosses
Africa of the longest Nile that feeds the Mediterranean
Africa the sanctuary of unspoiled nature
Africa sagging to knees with hunger!
Attending to the lust of the powerful in disguise
Now bogged down by virus that kills mercilessly
The Blackman in peril and desperation
Think of the Blackman in peril.

Africa of slave trade and apathy
Africa of colonialism and dictatorship

---

[28] Is a type of hardwood popularly used by the famous Makonde people of
Sourhern Tanzania for sculpture. *Mpingo* may correctly be called Ebony.

Africa of the divide and rule epoch
With its relics wide spread
Africa of the disgraceful Apartheid
Africa that is cheated time and again
Look at the Blackman in peril.

Look at the Blackman in peril
Africa of the brain drain and illiteracy
Africa at the crossroads and confusion
As one phase of treachery discards the old skin
Like a snake discarding its scale on a weary leaf
Now the strangest of nightmares upon us
As the master opens the rear door
Globalization the ultimate nightmare
The struggle now that slippery and malicious.

The Bleeding Heart

The heart of man radiates joy
But at a corner it harbours misery
Bitterness and agony intertwined
Surfacing outbursts of outrage
With tears right from the heart.

Yet life is that sweet
With the bless of tears
That sheds and unloads
The load of unhappiness
Ushering in hope and wishes
That one would wish to ride
Like the horses of time.

Let the heart bleed

Let tears pour down
Washing down the poison
That inhabits the heart of man.

Cry strongly and freely
Though in the darkness of your room
Lest the kids hijack you
For their tears will pain you
And prolong the bitterness
Delaying the gift of tears
That heals and smoothes like oil
That finally elates your soul to joy.

The Bleeding Palestine

No amount of pressure
No amount of suppression
The evil one shall be defeated
If it is for the one God of Moslems, Allah
If it is for the one God of Christians
That the humankind cowardly
Preaches and abuses by deeds and words
The shedding blood shall not be in vain.

The bleeding Palestine an eyesore
A shame to humankind
That pretends pious and holly
While inflicting acute pain and suffering
In the name of security and Promised Land
The land of honey and milk
Pushing Palestinians to the periphery
And now the war that looms
Spreading like bush fire of the savannah.

History is witness
That justice shall prevail
Tears of the innocent a curse
That will eat through the bones
Crushing the pride and arrogance
That hatches misery
With tears washing the blessed soils
That belongs to the Almighty God
Not the sinful minds of our times.

To Muhamad and friends in Palestine
Your dreams our dreams
Your pain and suffering remains
Our shared lot both in prayer and deed
May God usher in peace
And justice that shall prevail
As the fight against the evil one is sustained
To the day of victory and forever.

"The Common Interests"

One thing remains permanent
Cemented with such strength and might
Prevailing for centuries
Changing characters
The colours and motion
Like chameleon in the Kalahari Desert.

For that reason
Savimbi was a Hero, a Freedom Fighter!
Flashed in prestigious papers
In New York and Paris

Honoured to pose with Reagan
And indeed the power that is.

Why the dust in Zimbabwe?
While Madagascar is in flame?
In such a deafening silence.

Why Congo now? Why Kinshasa now?
After 40 years of Mobutu
A darling of the west?
A replacement? A suiting figurehead?
That never worked with Kabila
Who flashed semblance of Lumumba?
The immortal?

Mother Africa, with you we cry
Fumbling to fight the monster
That keeps crawling with viciousness
Spitting Vernin and poison
Shrouded in sweets and chocolate
Lest we forget, and only recently
A debate stirred in Canada
Labelling Mandela a terrorist
Though he remains a symbol
Of humility and humanity.

Let's remain focused, staring intently
At what bounds "them" together
Glued inseparably
In their doctrine and pursuit
To defend "The Common Interests".

The Crawling Africa

The crawling Africa
  Creeping in pace and front
Downtrodden for centuries and time
Exploited not only in blood and gold
But in credibility and mantle
Devoured like a carcass by vultures
The birds of strong beak and claws
With grip so hard and piercing.

The crawling Africa
Used for free in centuries
with soldiers of repute in wars
But relegated to oblivion and shame
phased to periphery like trash
like the ocean tides and filth.

The crawling Africa
Without voice in the absence of the master
The continent shaking in violence and fear
Her riches squandered in daylight
Robbed of its virtue by tricks and intrigues
And now the casualty of globalization!

The crawling Africa
with such a potential
Awash with resources and inertia
But bogged down by greed
not only by the aliens
but brothers of blood and caste
now clad with the masters gown
Ruling in impunity and muscle.

The crawling Africa

orphanage with the passage of time
with her heroes buried deep in soil
Lumumba who died in honour for Africa
but in pain and anguish
In the hands of brutal imperialists
With Nyerere, "the shining lamp put off"
A century gone for Africa.

The crawling Africa
With Nelson Mandela the lone voice
Though of age and retirement
reminding us of Mkwawa and Mirambo
Shaka and Steve Biko our icons
the continent laments of their passage
As Africa wades in deep hostile waters
With the campus misplaced
and the captain in deep slumber
GOD HELP AFRICA.

The Day of Reckoning

Time clicks and edges to darkness
Despair grips the most astute of all
With silence hurting and painful
As history recoils angrily
Like a hungry African python.

With lies that never lasted time
With malice that hurts the globe
Doctored espionage and sham
Now surfacing in bursts of shame
With the day of reckoning beckoning.

Witch hunting the project of waste
As hate steers the globe to ditch
The gift of life trodden with might
As muscle and weaponry prevail
With the darkest of hours imminent.

The day of reckoning in the offing
With the Britons weeping for Kelly
Across Atlantic smoke simmering
God forbade bloodletting
The day of reckoning signalling.

Time heals and hurts
With ugly revelations that shock
In time the treachery embedded
Since Karl Peters and the like
The pattern ever the same.

The Deafening Silence!

The drum bits sounding
The unfamiliar siren tormenting the ears
The melody not as soothing
The call of war now preoccupation
And what a war!

Waging a war not a piece of cake
War maims and inflicts terror
Hiroshima to date remains such a pain
With the world realigning now
Polarization as eminent
The aftermath to be horrific.

Failure of sense such a shame
The deafening silence such a menace
Nations of statute relegated to coma
Men and women of repute rendered imbecile
As the iron fist and arrogance reigns
With the obsession for war
Now such a painful thorn in the flesh.

The show of power and weaponry
The giants flexing muscles
Others with pillage of forbidden weapons
Nuclear warheads ready for assembly
Biological weapons of mass destruction
Researched in laboratories of death
What perverted minds of humankind!
Nelson Mandela broke the silence
His voice echoing resolutely
Typical of his boldness and high spirits
Telling what a villainy the superpower is
Germany has recounted the horrors of holocaust
France honouring its stately obligation
While Albion clings to her irritating loyalty
And yet the silence so deafening.

The Dream

A t last it came
The vividly horrifying dream
That kept me all awake
Like a child victim to malaria fever.

I mingled in my bed
Pondering what the dream meant

And a sad fact dawning onto me
That the hope of living was gone
Vanishing never to come back.

Those moving sounds of torture
They pierced through me
Like a nail through a soft wood
An overpowering covering the sky
And it all turned blood red
Is it symbolic of blood and death?

But yet there was that beautiful
spot
Amid standing a beautiful tree
Green and living amidst hell
Oh! Almighty God
Why torture me all this
It is past the tolerance limit
Overwhelming and painful
Give me a way out
Lest I collapse and fail
To render the message known
To your people, the world over.

The sky turned pinkish
All down the spectral beauty of
colour
The colours so lovely, reassuring
Oh! Thank you God
For giving me the beauty of colour.

But yet there it was again
The blood red sky
And amid stood the beautiful tree
Hissing voices filtering through
From the swaying leaves of beauty.

I sat in my bed
In the verge of tears and laughter
For I was frightened
Frightened by the ghostly dream
Though now I understand
Beyond the slightest blemish
That the beautiful flower
Stood there glittering
Green and healthy
For the ray of hope.

Yes, I understand
Peace shall come
But blood first!
Oh! Fate
And, Peace Forever.

The Evil Empires

Once upon a time the wind of change blew
The colonial masters holding breath
The tide irresistible and so forceful
Patriotic sons of Africa vocal and daring
Sons of the soil burning with vision.

Once upon a time the world traumatized
With Hitler obsessed to rule with muscle
Jews suffering the wrath of evil mind
Gas chambers scattered afar
Cold blood murder the pride of sick minds.

Once upon a time the globe that polarized
Cold war the verdict and litmus test
Affiliation the choice of necessity

Both in attire and posture
With sense defeated by overtones.

Once upon a time the axis of evil discovered
The master now that determined
With the anger burning ferociously
With a strategy to pursue that dates decades
Now the dream comes true
Regime change the latest invention.

Evil empires the snag of our times
With memories of our heroes resurfacing
Patrice Emery Lumumba tortured
His bones melted in acid like specimen
Flamboyant Mobutu climbing to throne
Letting the master reach
Down to the bowels of the earth.

Evil empires driven by desires
That quenching is such a nullity
Applauded even the shameful Apartheid
Now new terrains emerging
Disguised in jargons of merry vocabularies
Globalization and global initiatives.

The Fantasies of Capitalism

The bottom line inspirational
The profit equation sinking that low
Selling weapons of mass destruction
Fashionable and such a lucrative venture
Agitating for war
To open new horizons, new frontiers.

Profits the engine of growth
Overtrading erodes the capacity to prosper
Window dressing sending shock waves afar
With the giants of history gasping for air
Business failures en mass
Now the new formula sought by heart.

Agitating for war a new frontier
New theories of shame hatched
War holding a key for inertia
Destroy to reconstruct
Demolish and plan a new
Enhancing the bottom line
The capitalistic trash!

The pattern remains ever the same
But now so ferocious
With global hallucination in our midst
Globalization and *dot.com* economy
With the looming war of disguise
Meant to hold the absolute arsenal
The weapon to silence the market
The oil monopoly that has divided the world
And monopoly that was so loathed by
Adam Smith, the mentor of market forces.

The brunt of the messy to befall the poor
The struggling lots of Africa and Diasporas
Cleaning the debris of the wreckage
With exploitation spree on unabated
To quench the fantasies of capitalism
The bottom lines swelling to the brim
Awaiting the next phase of ruinous destruction
With the suffering to continue, a vicious circle!

The Forgiving Africa!

Africa of scars and wounds
Others still fresh and bleeding
With broken hearts and tearful eyes
Of traumatic history and tales.

The painful slave trade of shame
That robbed the continent of its inertia
Exposing the elderly to misery
Leaving the hearts with sorrow
And children to the merciless hyenas
That roamed to harvest
Without remorse or guilt.

Then came the balkanization
The shameful scramble for Africa
As a carcass devoured by vultures
With salivating ugly mouths
That remains as wide today.

The land conquered in earnest
Our ancestors phased to periphery
To aridity and barren stone
To perish and languish in thirst
Working for the brutal masters
Colonialists from the west.

Our ancestors perished in gunpowder
Mkwawa, Mirambo and Shaka
Then came Lumumba of intellect
Stive Biko of courage and wisdom
All devoured by the imperialists
As ugly Apartheid took root
Supported by the west.

As the sins of land grab persists
Mugabe perceived the evil one
Touching the untouchables
With Ian Smith still living
happily.

The masters now in honeymoon
As the style changes
The patterns evolving
Pitying African leaders against
each other
As if a bunch of fools
What a mockery and shame
The forgiving Africa!
Now a laughing stock!

"The Geneva of Africa"

Arusha the hub of action
People in elegant suits and
badges
People smiling and hurrying
Flycatchers abound
Shouting, *Jambo, Jambo!*[29]
Karibu!

Within a stones throw
The roof of Africa towers
Snowy and beautiful
Despite the perceived scotching
heat
Of the midday sun, along the
equator.

---

[29]   *Jambo, Jambo! Karibu!*..........................

The relic of Arusha Declaration
A monument of fame and name
With Mwalimu stamp left vividly
Though in ashes of history
Arusha historical and memorable
The home of *Zinjanthropas*[30]
The mother of mankind.

The foot of creation
Listed in the wonders of the world
The astounding Ngorongoro Crater
Amazing Serengeti migrations
Nature at its best.

Arusha the boiling pot
Arusha home to the world
With peace sought by heart
Conventions and congress in progress

Here mankind converges
Praying for the injured world
That bleeds and smells of injustice
Hatched of greed and lust for power.

Arusha of sirens for the powerful
Arusha of sirens for perpetrators
Of genocide and mass killing
Arusha the pride of Tanzania
And now crowned and indeed befitting
"THE GENEVA OF AFRICA".

---

[30] *Zinjanthropas* ....

The Geneva of Geneva

Not the Geneva of Africa
Now in the Geneva of Geneva
The hub of action
With people busy as bees
Scouting for hotel rooms
And often in vain.

Aboard Swiss Air
Hovering above the roof of Africa
Touching down the Nyayo land
Ready for the maiden trip
To the Geneva of Geneva
Leaving behind greenery
The splendour of creation
Above the clouds
Mingled with the sandy dust
Of the vast Sahara desert
The African landmark in air.

Zurich a step to Geneva
Scaling down the Alps
With the black forest imposing below
Spots of townships sandwiched
And beauty so spectacular.

Geneva the home to the world
Rainbow of colours apparent
From the Chinese
To the Bushmen of Kalahari
The envy of the Geneva of Africa.

Similarities, Yes
But dissimilarities stack clear too

And here we sell Tanzania
Wishing to bring the world to Tanzania
The Land of Kilimanjaro and Zanzibar.

The Inhuman Human

The saddest of times upon humanity
The ugliest of scenarios now unfolding
As wisdom leaves room to muscle
The mighty and powerful pounding
Human concern a mockery
Satisfying the ego such an obsession
Elation bone of the scale of ruinous attacks.

Human casualty not a concern
Piercing cries of children the music of time
The luminous skies the gift of souls
With laser guided missiles hitting the markets
Cities flattened to be rebuilt
Smoking the villainy from their hide outs
Liberating the people by killing en masse!
Killing to win the souls and hearts
What a tragedy to humanity?

Swift and surgical was the blue print
Hordes of refugee awaited in vast tents
The result so horrifying and painful
As confusion now reins with accusation
Sons and daughters of land betrayed
Now in slaughter houses and engulfed
With mothers shedding tears in anguish
Though the masters revenge in impunity
The world so shocked and in awe

As peace is sought by killing the innocent!

Think of the history of humankind
Dictatorship and apathy inscribed in fire
Saddam Hussein then the darling and partner
But now the evil one and the pain to humankind
Dictators created, propelled and crowned
As heroes both in time and space
Angels and Immortals labelled terrorists
Mandela, Biko, and Mahatma Gandhi you mention.

The Irony of Our Times

I f times were invented
If times were moulded
Curved from the black *"Mpingo"*
With the skilful hands of the *"Wamakonde"*[31]
Then the call for redesign is now.

Time an arbiter
Yet time an absolute monster
For time is irreversible
Its mission down hill unparalleled
To the ocean of fire
The turmoil in making.

Our time the peak of prosperity
Science fictions realized
The universe conquered
With the aliens terrorized by might
Of technology and geniuses
But leading to anguish

---

[31]   *"Wamakonde"* ....

The pain of our time.

Let men of wisdom speak
Let women of wisdom roar to life
Rebuking the perverted minds
Bent to breeding pain
Brought about by war and terror
With brunt leveled to the weak
The children and widowed mothers
Whose tears water the earth daily
But to no avail.

Cursed is our time
Though abundantly blessed
With wealth and ideals
With virtual revolution apparent
But tainted by greed
In hurry to destroy and inhibit
In the name of confusion
May God absolve humankind.

The Jungle Out There!

The jungle out there
The terrain that scare
With scorpions and vices
With intricate cobwebs that snare.

The jungle out there
The journey that never ends
With hope and wishes
With fear that simmers
The jungle out there!

The jungle out there
The sun that never sets
With treachery and malice
With hideous mischief
The jungle out there!

Yet life that sweet
Despite the jungle out there!
With hyenas of appetite
With the scorpions that bite.

The jungle out there!
The cardinal rule of time
With the scotching heat
Of the sun that burn
Or of the freezing glaciers
Of the poles that position the earth.

The jungle out there!
Shrubs and thorny trees
With the birds of wing sparring
The hawks of claws hunting
The scavengers on the look
The jungle out there!
Careful!

The Lustful Heart

The lustful heart of man speaks
The lustful heart of man rules
Punching and pushing hard
To insanity with loathing
Trumping on life for greed
The insatiable urge of the flesh
Occasionally leading to misery
If not murderous death by design
All to satisfy the flesh.

Tame your lust my brother
Despite the beauty of legs
Close your eyes to romantic eyes
Heal the heart with courage
Lest it leads you to anguish
To the painful soul for betrayal
As insatiable urge remains potent
Inviting agony from the vice
The virus ruining life
Disguised in a pursuit to happiness.

The lustful heart plunges one to
bondage
Now acquiring scary dimensions
The body immunity impaired
As HIV-AIDS sets in
Engaging the blood warriors to battle
A merciless war that is never won!

No protection, not the best of shields
Of sophistication and technology
Not the finest of membranes
Matches the brutal virus
That is poised to kill

With precision and accuracy
But taming the lustful heart.

The Malicious Mind

The roots of havoc and suffering
The seeds of provocation and chaos
The turmoil of humankind history
Springs from the perverted mind
That hatches mischief
Born of malice by design.

The sin of malice has pervaded history
Manifesting itself in colour and race
Camouflaging as pious religion
In the name of one God
Who discriminates among his subjects!
What a contradiction!

Down the memory lane
Even King David hatched malice
Taking life to cool his lust
Planning shamelessly with greed
Driven by the perverted mind
That remains mischievous.

In commerce and agriculture
In science and fiction
Man orchestrates hideous ideas
Bent on inflicting pain and misery
All planed meticulously
Malice the driving engine.

The malicious mind an abomination
Justifying wars and shame
Throwing the globe to an apparent ruin
A formidable expedition to extinction
From diseases and smoking guns
With the nuclear Armageddon lingering.

The Maniacs of War

The Maniacs of War
  Talking of war?
The war talk has ambushed civilization
As if war the price of life
As if war the wonder jewel
That captivated the souls and minds
Of the sailors, the pirates of high seas.

Talking of war?
The history of war the shame of humankind
War not a crown for the sober minds
For war will torment the mind
For war has never been won in history
But its relics and vestiges the eyesores
That remain vivid in the path of history.

Talking of war?
The history of mankind full of war maniacs
The misfits of time dreaming of war and terror
Their pleasure the wreckage and shaded blood
Thirsty for war running down their veins
Always throwing the world to the darkest of times.

Talking of war?

War always a misconception
With rhetoric pumped to the young and agile
But after war limping and confused
With anger and retribution burning
Cursing their being and essence
While the architects of war enjoy in retirement
Going to the annals of history unscratched
Their children running the giants of commerce
Managing the reconstruction
Negotiating the most lucrative of deals
The spoils of war the reserves for success.

Talking of war?
What a shameful embankment!
With the globe now torn apart
Petrol prices now skyrocketing
The brunt now borne by the poor
With the future so bleak, so insecure.

The Misery of HIV/AIDS

The misery of HIV/AIDS
The history of humankind
Is awash with traumatic upheavals
With plaque and small pox outbursts
As heads rolled with vicious attacks
Vaccine sought with resolve
Fear gripping the populations.

Life always on a delicate balance
With eminent scourges of famines
With wars fought to destroy
While diseases erupting with vengeance

In rebellion against mans misdeeds.

Then the final crunch
The final assault in action
With the body immunity paralysed
The body vitality drained
Flesh parting with bones
Coughing that terrorizes, the order of day
With stigma and isolation
Adding to the aggression and misery.

HIV-AIDS the menace of our times
Touching the softest of parts
And afflicting all
Regardless of age and mantle
Not even fearful of fame or function.

HIV-AIDS transcends colours and repute
Suffocating to death
Even the mighty and powerful
As they all lust with erotic fantasies
Searching for the heights of orgasm
Dreaming of eternal bliss
That now HIV-AIDS has shattered.

The misuse, the misdeed
Typical of the destructive man
Turning the gift of life to prostitution
Commercializing even the holiest of deeds
With this misery upon us now
Deserving even a dedication, a day in calendar
What a shame to humankind.

The Nuclear Holocaust

It is neither the launchers
Nor the nuclear warheads
It is not the nuclear submarines
Not even the fastest of warplanes
That breeds fear and terror.

Nuclear holocaust sits
Complacently and leisurely
In the heart of man.

It will only take
The head of a crazy man
With ambition akin to stupidity
With the lowest of IQs[32]
With the lust for power
In hurry to rule the globe
Dictating terms and norms
As if the Maker of Mankind.

Nuclear holocaust now in lips
A topical issue for discussions
By the super powers that are
In fear of the loner with beard
With the urge to press the button
And blow the globe in smoke and dust.

---

[32]   IQ ....

Look!
It is the perverted mind
The heart with hatred
Dreaming of engulfing the world
In an evil grip
That should scare mankind most.

It is the selfish ego
Of the exploitation spree of history
That man loves and craves for
Not only recently, not only now
But for centuries and time
That mankind should fear most.

The Riches of the Earth

The riches of the earth
The demise of the earth
The earthly vice and greed
The ground for rebellion.

The riches of the earth
The engine of growth
The growth of industry
The Vernon of the earth.

The riches of the earth
In the bowels of the earth
With gold and diamond
With copper and metalloid
With tears and blood.

The riches of the earth
The seamless vaults of wealth
The wealthy with teeth
To Scramble with filth.

The riches of the earth
The path of death
With gold and tanzanite
The rarity of time
The gift of generations.

The riches of the earth
The seat of faith
With tax and lottery
With treachery and robbery.

The Shadow of Death [33]

In the darkness of a great forest
Lies my price and honour
In the pool of blood
Dwell my most beautiful dreams.

Through the thorny forest
My path wanders to wilderness
Among the cries of agony
Is the rose of my soul.

Oh! See my beloved brothers
See through the forest of ignorance
The forest of torture and oppression
Of the black man in peril.

---

[33]   The Shadow of Death.....................................

Oh! Come see mankind
Of this abuse and insult
Of humanity and integrity.

Oh! Come blind world
Come blacks and whites
Come all bodies and souls
Come angels from the heaven
And see the abuse of mankind.

But he who dies lives
Though in the shadow of death
The candle of hope glows strong.
(*January 1988*)[34]

The Shame of Hunger

The dark pages unfolding
The world once again hit by shame
Of the moving skeletons
With souls and life
But wavering and swaying
Of hunger and deadly thirst.

"*We're the World*"
"*We're the Children*"
[35]Renowned artists of the world saw it then
Sung bit with passion and love
Urging the rich to reconsider
And cleanse the world of the shame.

---

34 ....
35 ....

The world swimming in wealth and affluence
Conspicuous consumption a pattern
The world in a spending spree
With wasteful spoils of value
While other roam animal naked
Sagging to knees not in prayer
But in pain of hunger and thirst.

Yet resources committed
To weaponry and agitation
For war and oppression
If not supremacy and segregation
With fingers hurriedly pointed
And accusations abound
For the exploited Africa
Reeling now in pains
Of the history of shame and greed
That keeps changing colours
Like the chameleons of the Kalahari.

The Signs of Time

Time the cure of times
The future shrouded in time
With the present disgusting and scary
Our past the trail of terror.

The signs of time that gloomy
With star wars simulated with precision
The talent of brains devoted to Armageddon
While humanity recalls the pain of small pox
The bouts of pandemic that swept the globe

Now SARS[36] shivery and anxiety
While HIV/AIDS entrenches itself stubbornly.

The signs of time predictable
Man against man the historical shame
From the crude Stone Age weaponry
To the gunpowder that swept Aborigines
With the conquest of Africa for her riches
Weapons of mass destruction now in wrong reach.

The signs of time that revealing
Civilization at the cross road
Mother nature also running amok
Earth tremors claiming in abundance
With astrologists depicting collision in universe
The final crunch in making.

Time the arbiter
The signs of times sending shock waves
Poverty spreading like bush fire
Conspicuous consumption overwhelming a handful
With death in staggering proportions
Malnutrition in the midst of plenty.

The signs of time that revealing
The suffering given myriad of justifications
The curse of the biblical distortion
The cure prescribed in bitter doses of rhetoric
Pillars evolving to sustain the malice
The signs of time that gloomy.

---

[36] A diseas reported after bird flue.....................................

Soul-searching Episode

My soul wonders in the wilderness, vastness
Counting the species that change my gasps
Enticing my being for the fortunes that glitter
Crying for the embraces, that turns sour
My dreams unfolding only to encounter betrayal.

Seated under the baobab tree, in search of a shade
My heart palpating with beats that scare even self
With the shear size and volume, though without shade
The big hearted baobab tree just a specie
A wonder in the jungle
To soothe etching back of elephants.

My thirst left unabated, with scorching sun and heat
With confusions mounting in fear
Life crumbling on my feet and muscles so painful
My soul left asunder, wondering in the wilderness.

Out in the cities with glass and debris
With bureaucracy that inhibits not only inertia
But injustice that will ruin the nation
Inviting even cluster bombs, disguised to liberate
My heart burning with bile
As clumsy clouds linger, suffocation the souls
That remain wondering with species
Awash in the wilderness
That souls roam in futile.

Down to the deep seas
With stories of whales and sharks
Though dolphins usher in hopes
Pirates roam with swords
May be universe the cure?
Though alien in their galaxies

With science fiction so terrifying
My soul left in perplex
Wandering through the wilderness
The soul searching continue,
The episode of our times.

The Street Souls of Arusha

I f souls could be captured
Kept in the safe custody of cages
Nursed to grow with hearts
What a powerful nation
What a formidable force
That street children of the world is.

Thrown to the cold streets
Without mercy or remorse
As the lust of the flesh turns sour
Partners crawling at each other
Like the cruel wild cats
Affections turning to afflictions
The children rocked with fear
Jumping for asylum in the dirty
streets
Full of vice and virulence.

The street children of Arusha
Like the "*chokoraa*"[37] of Nairobi
A nightmare in the daylight
In the cities of the world
Now a force to reckon with
Participating in revolution!

---

[37] An alternative name used for street children particularly in Nairobi, Kenya.

The street souls
Bragging and begging
With tormenting stares and piercing eyes
But souls all the same
Bleeding with pain and hatred
But growing in height and muscle
To a formidable force of vengeance
That will rock Arusha to her knees
With this slumber and complacency.

The *Street Children* of Arusha
A curse and a blessing
Their souls part of our souls
Their dreams inseparably our dreams
Their nightmares ultimately ours.

The Sun

The morning sun
Its golden sky from the east
With its rays glittering
Offering richly
Its golden generosity.

The sun rises from its den
It hastens from its eastern horizon
Engulfing the world
In surprise and marvel.

The pleasure and security
Imparted in mankind

In the regularity and surety
Of the sun rise and fall
Which imparts new hopes
Revealing in style
The rich provisions of nature
And the maker.

Slowly it goes on
Over the cloudy sky and distance
Shining even brighter
Declaring the beautiful day
All laid before the man.

And eventually it darkens
Fading its brightness
From the sharp white
To the pale and yellow
And the golden colour again
Hidden to the far western horizon.

This is the novelty of life
As mar less as the snow
As smooth as the oil touch
And as warmly, as the motherly love.

And tomorrow again
As are many days to come
Even to the New Year
The rhythm persists
And amid this calm of peace
Of enchanting songs
Sung by birds of the bush
Of colour and curiosity
Given by flowers in the bush
The filthy hand sneaks in!

Then chaos reign
The hatred pricked
And violence the style.

Yet the sun gathers momentum
Maintaining its sacred expedition
Of morning and night
Of light and darkness
Of love and happiness.

This strange pattern of wit
The pattern of perfection
I love and adore
But yet I disrupt!

Oh me!
The cursed creature of the earth
I love and hate
I bless and curse
In the midst of havoc.

Yet I swear again
That tomorrow is coming
Because the sun is still there
With its tender symbolic voice
The voice of love and peace.

For colour is beauty
The morning scenery a bless
The golden sky my dream
Though a corrupt dream!

The Ugly Face of Death

*E*yes roll and stare in nakedness
　　Mouth twisted in a curve of
mockery
The body docile and stiff in posture
With limbs dry and cracking
The ugly face of death so shocking.

Whether the body in the streets of
Baghdad
Death reminiscent of gushing bullet
wounds
Of the insatiable pursuit of riches in
Africa
Or from the debris of the flattened
twin towers
Be it from the capital penalty of
shame
Death remains ugly and disgusting.

Death remains ugly and disgusting
Be it of a terrorist or a saintly
pretender
Eyes will roll and stare in nakedness
Till humanly gesture attends the
eyelids
Gently attending the yawning mouth
Hiding the smile that never was.

Death the gate way to eternity
Though instilling fear and uproar
As piercing cries of moaning fill the
air
Bodies lying in limbo and merry

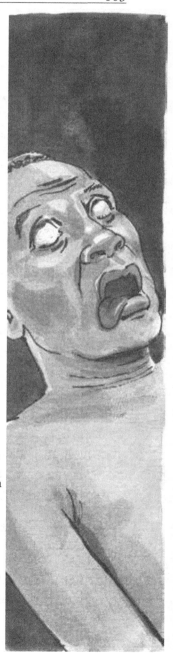

caskets
While others rot out in the bushes of Bunia
This is the irony of our times.

The Unholy Trinity

Think of the pattern of life
Think of the Twin Towers and Pentagon
Think of the axis of evil in triplet
Life full of triple affliction.

Think of the pattern of events
Even the formula of salvation!
The Holy Biblical trinity
The Father, Son and The Holy Spirit
Now abused by the war mongers.

Think of the fear unleashed
Aggressors poised for a catapult
The trial neglecting the world appeal
That war not the best of acts
But the mother of all pains.

Think of the unholy trinity in making
Bush, Blair and the Spanish fellow
Making a mockery of the world
Loathful of war, blood hounds of our times
Hiding behind another unholy trinity
Iraq, Iran and the confident Korea
Poised to fulfil unholy trinity?

Think of the unholy desires
Think of the innocent cries of the children

Not only in the streets of Baghdad
But also the aftermath
The suffering to befall Africa
With the unholy trinities
That now baffle humankind

The Vicious Mind

The mind of man is mischievous
Wondering in the wildest of dreams
Pondering to inflict the severest of pains
Nabbing the budding flowers
The rising stars a pain in the flesh.

Despite the time and age
The sick mind will persist
Wishing life could be reduced to rubble
Though old age persisting like glue
Fighting with time though in futile
As fatigue and slow pace take hold
Wishing for the time reversal
That remains as elusive
Shifting like mirage on the long road.

The vicious mind of man persists
Venturing to the realms of dark powers
That is rife with treachery
Which invariably leads to mental touchier
Poverty crawling with vengeance
As the mind remain captive.

Finally the sick mind seeks recourse
To the ultimate weapon of vicious mind
Dreaming the sickliest of all deeds

Murder, bloodletting and sacrifice
To quench the quest for greed
That time never healed down the history
Despite the gift of life and age.

Life and death the treasured gifts of man
To live and die the honour of time
For celebrities and the down trodden
Life and death the inevitable choice
That is crowned and graced by life
Lived with clean heart and humility.

The War front - HIV and AIDS

The nation at war
The world in a nasty battlefield
With its soldiers injured
Limping of heavy causalities.
The territory is infiltrated
By unsuspecting messengers of death
First disguised as "slim"
Ghostly people from there
After the bloody *Amin War*.

The amour at hand terrifying
As it breaks the front from within
Instilling deficiency and havoc
While incapacitating defence
However sophisticated it may be.

This is a war front
Calling for solders of repute
Of both will power and hardware

Resolve and care
The genesis notwithstanding
The enemy is upon us
Engulfing the nation in panic
Paralysing even the mightiest of all.

HIV-AIDS deeply entrenched
As it afflicts the softest of parts
Threatening the very essence of living
What "*Mzee Ruksa*"[38], of wisdom
Expressed as "*Kitumbua chaingia mchanga*"[39]
Adding "*Gonjwa limeingia pabaya*".

Now, though late
But better late than not
The war declared
With generals appointed
Lets pray for victory.

Though So Gloomy, Yet So Reassuring

As the globe edges to the darkest of times
As the rift widens for the call of rationale
As the vessels to spat the Vernon remain poised
Frustrations mounting for the masters
A ray of hope shines from afar
Humanity speaking in unison
Mammoth demonstration the world over
So reassuring are the voices
Filling the streets of this terrified globe.

Though so gloomy, yet so reassuring
People speaking though in vain

[38] Mzee Ruksa.....................................
[39]

As the crooked ones maintain an evil grip
Propelling the world to the Armageddon
Disregarding the sensible gestures
The cries for peace and harmony
As if intoxicated with a ruinous wine
That erodes the commonest of wisdom
That war an abomination and not a blessing.

Congratulations the world masses
For the placards of wisdom and courage
Condemning war and its perpetrators
Joining hands with the noble leaders of time
The crusaders of peace even in turmoil
Singing dialogue and humanly philosophy
Paving the way for understanding and
Respect for the already heavily bleeding planet!

Though so gloomy, yet so reassuring
People matching in hordes and appealing silence
People singing for peace
Despite ridicule by Howard and his likes
People mourning bitterly for those to be maimed
While others in tears for their sons and daughters
Being sent to slaughter houses in the Gulf
In the name of war shrouded with a mystery
War defying logic if not common sense.

Touring the Empire

Remnants of slavery the first leg
Apartheid relic the seat of empire
With agenda that tally ambition
Though Africa relegated to irrelevance
Africa tour the blemish of shame.

Bow to the master the shame of time
The stripping of royal table
Lures the modern stooges of Africa
Holding brethren in bondage
Impoverished, limping for centuries.
Permanent interest not a folklore
The riches of Africa there to harvest
History the witness to the trail of looting
From slavery to colonialism
And now the rediscovery and euphoria
Corporate tentacles the *modus operandi.*

Then the beads and rolls of garment
If not the smoking riffles and ambush
With the icons of vision and revolution
Freedom fighters baptized terrorist
Imprisonment for life on a hoax
Now testimony of moral steadiness.

Africa on a treat for a malady
A plate of crocodile sympathy paraded
Paving way for the giants of commerce
The cancer of terrorism to remain away
Permanent interest not a folklore
The master touring the empire

Servants in a trembling spree
Saluting with earnest and awe
Awaiting with their watery mouths
For the master to drop the Biblical…!

But behold!
Mandela spoke with heart
Humanity now in trepidation
May God save our souls!

Tribute to Mwalimu

Birth and death are like twins
Those are at times separated
Not only by time and pain
But also distinction and label.

Julius Kambarage Nyerere
Adored and loved
Hated and feared
But recorded in the annals
Of history and mankind.

Thanks Almighty God
For the gift of Mwalimu
Who moulded Tanzania
While moulding his person
That left a glaring label
In Africa and the world.

In Zanaki land he was born

With his star shining bright and high
Not only for Zanakis, lest they boast!
But mankind at large
Though with painfully sharpened teeth
His wit was even more refined
Though he remained typically Zanaki
By birth to burial
Mwalimu towered higher than that.

As Mwalimu he taught
As a leader he led with vision
His convictions and determination
Stood clear of self and egoism.

Though his version of humanity
Failed the test of time
Crumbling hurriedly in Zanzibar
Upon the mighty muscle of capital
If not greed and thirst
Characteristic of mankind
He towers higher and higher.

That is why they came
People of age and fame
From all corners of the globe
The magnitude in rainbow colours
Spoken of by Mandela.

In South-South commission he left
A clear mark and contribution
That debts is power
A machete to wield
A potent weapon of negotiation.

In Tanzania he left

An adorable formula of succession
Crushing the myth of royal stigma
Leading now and proudly
To a third phase of government
Of democracy and ballot box
Not of chocolate and sweet
Dropped by the invisible masters.

They used to call him *Musa*![40]
Despite his dislike
Self appointed "*Kiranja*"[41]!
Though rightly so
As he led freedom fight
That stretched afar, from Mozambique
Namibia and Angola to Zimbabwe
Against Smith and white supremacy
Down south, from the shackles
Of Robben Islands of shame
With the release of Madiba
Nelson Mandela, the rock of patience.

In retirement that never was
The great lakes region he toured
Preaching peace and harmony
Among the crowd of wolves
Designed by the imperialists.

At AICC Mwalimu shined

---

[40]   Musa is a biblical name Mosses, leader of Jews who led the disgranted
       Jews from slavery in Egypt only to wonder in the deserts for so many
       years. Wheres, some were fond of using the analogy to Mwalimu, the
       founding president of Tanzania, it is said he never liked it at all.
[41]   *Kiranja* School headboy used on mMwalimu with the same conotation
       to his dislike.

With his "*Kifimbo*"[42] held lightly, loosely
Looking fragile and angered
By the irreconcilable brothers of tongue
Called Tutsis and Hutus
In their *Burundi Peace Negotiations*.[43]

Finally Mwalimu succumbed
To the inevitable but cowardly death
That never thinks of pain and bitterness
It inflicts among the people.

This is a tribute to Mwalimu
Remembering his birth day
And indeed the death
That never managed to wipe out
His share, his contributions to mankind
Happy birthday Mwalimu
In Heaven and Peace.

Unending Turmoil

At times it is like a movie
Images flying in patches
Guns of make on display
Roaring machine guns that aim
With precision and targets
And oceans doted with weaponry.

Smoking the villains from hideouts

---

[42] *Kifimbo* a stick, but not a ordinary one, but rather a stick like ones carried by African Chiefs to symbolize authority.

[43] Refers to the protracted negotiation at AICC between the warring fuctions of Burundi, Hutus and Tuts, reconciled by Mwalimu and later on Nelson Mandela following the death of Mwalimu.

Patriotic young lions out to serve
Giving human kind a glimpse of light
From regimes that terrorize
Evil empires of patronage
That created monsters we cry foul of.

At times it is like a movie
The unending turmoil of grieve
With blood letting and death
Innocent patriots misguided
With children scattered in fear
As terrorists hit and run
Back to their holes and castles
That lither the globe.

The unending turmoil of grief
Euphrates's and Tigris crying
Ancient civilizations lamenting
Replaced by land mines that explodes
Maiming even the angels.

Euphrates and Tigris crying
The yawning vacuum evident
Is the ghost with moustache underground?
Or gone with the blast of blister bombs?
A million pound question!
As the make shift government stammer
Even the master transfixed.

What a Shame for Africa! Burundi

*D*espite the facts of history
Of the Africa split and scramble
Of the Berlin gathering of wolves
The divide and rule device
That colonialists employed
Planting the seeds of war
Leaving behind skirmishes
Rebellion among brothers
Burundi smacks of shame.

What a shame for Africa
Brother devouring brother
In cold blood and vengeance
Sisters scheming in earnest
For the death of own sisters
Enmity boiling to brim
The counsel by leader ridiculed
Sitting to the dead of the nights
Arbitrating in futile.

Mwalimu dreamed of peace
Devastating own health with sympathy
Parting in grief for failure
To reconcile the irreconcilable
The brothers of tongue.

Madiba, Mandela the icon of will power
Cried for their insensitivity
Their love for chauffeur driven limousines
With their kids studying in Brussels
While the people perish in bush
Fighting a stupid war
As the so called leaders
Shuttle the world cities

In immaculate suits with purses
Full of dollars, shillings if not rands
What a shame for Africa.

Winning the Hearts and Minds

Amid hearts that bleed so profusely
   Amid the sorrowful souls, wandering minds
Amid havoc and chaos in making
With hospital equipment on the streets
With anarchy taking root in earnest
The blatant rhetoric echoes
The time of liberation is now
Winning hearts and minds the pious mission.

Let the chaos escalate
For chaos breeds freedom!
Let knife-wielding youths wander resiliently
Now the symbols of liberated Baghdad!
The globe staring in awe and shock
As winning of hearts and minds continue.

Down with the weapons of mass destruction
The song that changed melody so swiftly
Terror links to be impaired permanently
Reaching to the people under tyranny
Restoring the peace and freedom
Though with causalities reeling with pain
The "collateral damages" of war
Winning the hearts and minds in style.

The message loud and clear
Not even the strongest to sustain the vigil

The firepower from the master the language
The world now destined to the wilderness
With the map confiscated by the master
With muscle and arrogance apparent
Out to win the hearts and minds!

The new world order in place
The Britton Woods rejuvenated
The pillars mounted on such a foundation
With death toll for innocent so terrifying
Though without monuments to remember
The master out to win the hearts and minds
Leaving behind the scars never to heal
Though opening the earth bowels
For the ultimate price of war!

Wishes Awash

I f wishes were horses, to ride astride
In times of honey moon, or waves of tides
One would scale the moon, if not the Mars
Exploring the universe, if not the baboons
If wishes were horses, every one would ride.

If wishes were horses, to ride astride
One would wish to ride, floating with ease
Walking on oceans, like the biblical tale
Or conquering empires, with the ease of sword
That life is, the pain and anguish
If wishes were horses, every one would ride.

If wishes were horses, to ride astride
Without even the saddles, to comfort the rider

Or the remorse soul, to leak the wounds
Now bleeding anew, corroded with saline
That inhabits in spirits, the heart of man
If wishes were horses, every one would ride.

If wishes were horses, to ride astride
To flirt and flow, in bliss like Solomon
Or fly and flower, like the butterflies of beauty
If wishes were horses, every one would ride.

If wishes were horses, to ride astride
Life would vanish like smoke, bellowing
below
Like David decreed, to kill in malice
For the lust of the flesh, beauties abound
If wishes were horses, every one would ride.

Yes, Nujoma the Voice of Africa

Divide and rule the old gimmick
    Set in practice in Berlin
The vestiges still voiced
That Nujoma not the voice
Oh no, not the voice of Africa!

The old trick still ticking
Nujoma couldn't speak for Africa
A cherished ideal for the west
One voice for Africa a threat
And who else could voice it better?
If not Blair for the pack
The deacon of colonialism

The perpetrator and the mentor
Of the latest strategy
The deadliest weapon of all
Now called "*global Apartheid*".

Printed in the United States
by Baker & Taylor Publisher Services